# THE SHORTER POEMS

OF

# WALTER SAVAGE LANDOR

WALTER SAVAGE LANDOR

by WILLIAM FISHER

# THE SHORTER POEMS

OF

# WALTER SAVAGE LANDOR

SELECTED AND EDITED

BY

## J. B. SIDGWICK

CAMBRIDGE
AT THE UNIVERSITY PRESS
1946

# CAMBRIDGE
## UNIVERSITY PRESS

University Printing House, Cambridge CB2 8BS, United Kingdom

Published in the United States of America by Cambridge University Press, New York

Cambridge University Press is part of the University of Cambridge.

It furthers the University's mission by disseminating knowledge in the pursuit of education, learning and research at the highest international levels of excellence.

www.cambridge.org
Information on this title: www.cambridge.org/9781107635210

First published 1946
First paperback edition 2014

*A catalogue record for this publication is available from the British Library*

ISBN 978-1-107-63521-0 Paperback

# CONTENTS

*To*

KAY'S MEMORY

# INTRODUCTION

L ANDOR occupies an anomalous position in the hier-
   archy of English letters: occupies it with an air partly
   of arrogant disdain, partly of serene and clear-sighted
confidence. The anomaly lies in the conflict between his true
stature as a superb prose writer, and his treatment at the
hands both of his contemporaries and of posterity. Landor,
though he lived through the white-hot years of the Romantic
revival, showed himself in all his work to be one of the most
unaffectedly classical writers of the English heritage. The
immense span of his life—he was born in 1775, lived to see
Swinburne on his knees before him in sincere if embarrassing
homage, and died in 1864—had its leaping-off point in the
age of Richardson, Sterne and Johnson; and thence arched
across the years to encompass such alien elements as
Browning, Tennyson, Dickens, the Lake poets and the pre-
Raphaelites. But it was the classical spirit that inspired him,
and to which he gave his lasting love; from his earliest youth,
Pope, Milton and the Greeks were his idols, and he followed
them with unswerving devotion to the grave. Landor's
classicism was no mere parading of belvederes, gazebos,
faked ruins, and the rest of the Augustan knicknacks: the
contemporary of the great Romantic poets, he was not of
them. He was, rather, the ugly duckling of the Romantic
revival.

From his childhood until his last days in Florence, Landor
poured forth a steady stream of lyrics and occasional verses,

7

poetic dramas and prose pieces. Even in his own time he was not a writer to attract the multitude, the early nineteenth-century equivalent of the lending library subscribers of to-day. His outstanding qualities were not of an order to appeal to the mass of the reading public, then or now. Essentially, as Mr A. L. Rowse has recently remarked, he was a writer's writer, and his achievements were recognised and praised by such diverse and discriminating critics as Isaac D'Israeli, Hazlitt, Southey, Browning, De Quincey, Dickens and Wordsworth. But none recognised more clearly than Landor himself that he would always be more praised than read: 'I shall dine late', he said, 'but the dining-room will be well lighted, the guests few and select.' Elsewhere he wrote: 'I claim no place in the world of letters; I am alone, and will be alone, as long as I live, and after.'

To-day he is virtually unread. Dorothy Parker neatly summarises the matter in *A Pig's Eye View of Literature*:

> Upon the work of Walter Landor
> I am unfit to write with candour.
> If you can read it, well and good;
> But as for me, I never could.

Distinguished by outstanding intellectual powers, the master of an unparalleled prose style which reverberates and thunders in the reader's ear, a poet who could condense into four perfect lines the scattered bitterness of a lifetime, a political thinker whose enlightened and far-seeing detachment distinguished him from his contemporaries—Landor, despite all this, is to-day remembered for a few extracts from the *Imaginary Conversations*, in this anthology and that, and for one or two oft-recurring lyrics. Within the last fifteen years there has, indeed, been some indication of a slight revival of interest. The publication of the fine Chapman and

Hall *Complete Works*, during the years 1927–31, and the recent appearance of Malcolm Elwin's *Savage Landor* have done something to focus attention on one of the most unjustly neglected writers.

Not only as a writer, but as a man, Landor commands attention. It is again remarkable that one so vital, complex, wayward, passionate and tragic, a rebel by whose side Byron seems to posture too self-consciously, should have held so little interest for biographers. Into his eighty-nine years he crammed enough trouble, excitement, anger, love, vituperation and agony to stock a dozen more orthodox lives. From his earliest days a rebel and iconoclast, he was constantly in trouble with authority, indefatigably in arms against bureaucracy, against injustice, against organised and socially approved racketeering, incompetence and humbug.

His long and tumultuous life does not lend itself to effective treatment in a short sketch, but the salient events may be mentioned for the light which they throw upon certain recurrent themes in his poetry. A brilliant but erratic boyhood culminated in his expulsion from Rugby, his first serious clash with authority. Three years later he was rusticated from Oxford, exemplifying Sir Arthur Quiller-Couch's dictum that Cambridge makes dons of her poets, while Oxford, taking the healthier course, expels them.

At the age of twenty-eight Landor fell in love with Sophia Jane Swift, a young married Irishwoman who figures in many of his poems under the name Ianthe. Ianthe was probably the most enduring and powerful inspiration of his life, and for her he cherished a deep and tender affection which lasted until her death, forty-eight years later. .

In 1808, after more than a decade's aimless loving and writing and toying with politics, Landor bought Llanthony

9

Abbey, a fine property among the mountains of Monmouth-shire. In the same year began his lifelong friendship with Southey. For some months, too, he served as a volunteer in the Spanish insurgent army, to which cause also he gave financial help on a scale he could ill afford. Three years later he married Julia Thuillier and installed himself and his bride at Llanthony.

From the first they were beset by troubles. Landor was soon at war with the local authorities on the one hand, and with his Welsh neighbours and tenants on the other. The laziness, procrastination, dirt and dishonesty of almost every-one with whom he had dealings provoked his towering in-dignation and finally dragged him into a court case. A pair of rascally lawyers (Gabb and Gabell, who figure in two poems included in this collection) did nothing to ease the situation. In 1813 Landor's position had become insupport-able, and he fled to Swansea. In the following year a writ for libel was issued against him—at no period of his life did Landor show any interest in keeping the objects of his resent-ment ignorant of his feelings towards them—and, aware that he had technically no case whatever, he sailed for Jersey. There he was joined by his wife, and in 1815 they arrived in Italy, which was to be his home for the next twenty years. He never again set foot in Llanthony, upon which he had squandered a large part of his inheritance.

The next two decades, from 1815 to 1835, saw the slow consolidation of a limited but enviable reputation, and also the break-up of Landor's domestic background. He began to write and publish the *Imaginary Conversations*. He was visited by Hazlitt, and by Emerson, upon whose young mind he made an indelible impression. On his one visit to England he made or renewed the acquaintance of Southey, Lamb,

Coleridge and Wordsworth. During this early period of his life, Landor's energies were canalised into the *Imaginary Conversations*, and into massive verse dramas, of which *Gebir*, the most important, brought him some notice. But with the failure of *Gebir, Count Julian, and other Poems* in 1831, he ceased to regard himself seriously as a poet: but, although he never again turned his hand to the sonorous, turgid, unactable blank-verse dramas of his earlier years, his output of light occasional verse was unfailing to the end of his life. 'Poetry', he said, 'was always my amusement, prose my study and business.' Essentially patrician, despite his republican reputation, Landor never indeed regarded literature as a profession, but rather as an appropriate hobby for the gifted amateur.

A single incident from this period of his life illustrates, more forcibly than any reiteration, Landor's impulsiveness as well as his incorrigibly original view of things. He was keenly appreciative of the civilised delights of a good table, and the ineptitude of one of his Italian cooks frequently drove him near to despair. Being presented, one day, with an even less palatable dish than usual, Landor seized the perpetrator and pitched him through the window. A second later he dashed to it, and leaning out to observe the wretched cook lying with a broken limb in the flower-bed below, exclaimed, 'Good God! I forgot the violets.' Life with Landor, if interesting, could never have been easy. As a lady of his acquaintance once remarked: 'The great enjoyment of walking out with him had only one drawback, that he was always knocking somebody down.'

Landor being the man he was, his stay in Italy was not without its clashes with authority. Soon after his arrival, his outspokenness resulted in his expulsion from Como; and a *fracas* with the British minister at Florence, whom Landor loathed and imagined to have slighted him, all but led to a second expulsion. But of much graver concern than these skirmishings were the domestic developments which came to a head in 1835. His life, in retrospect, appears to us, as to Landor, to have been a series of howling blunders. And not least among them was his marriage to Julia Thuillier, a shallow, bitter, vicious woman, for whom it is impossible to believe he had ever felt such emotions as Ianthe had aroused in him. Julia had expected her marriage to ensure her two things: material comfort, and a position in the social world. The tragic farce of Llanthony deprived her of the former; Landor's refusal to play stool-pigeon to Gabb and Gabell, the latter. Without the buttress of a loved and loving husband, bitterness and estrangement were less surprising than inevitable.

· All this Landor bore without complaint, for he recognised the role that his own shortcomings had played in the disruption of the marriage. But when Julia began systematically to alienate the children (Arnold, the eldest, was born in 1818) from their father, then Landor revolted. Infidelity he tolerated, bitterness and recrimination he was inured against; but to remain at Fiesole and see his presence made the occasion for the perversion of his children and for his own humiliation was intolerable. Once again he uprooted himself, and returned to England.

Two years later, at the age of sixty-two, he settled at Bath, scene of many happy associations with Ianthe and his younger days, and his own home for the next twenty-one years.

Friendship and incessant activity were the keynotes of this third phase of his life. He met Dickens, he was visited by Carlyle and FitzGerald, and began his long friendship with

Browning. It is remarkable that despite his many foibles and his aggressive, uncompromising nature, Landor was, nevertheless, one of those rare spirits who are possessed of a genius for friendship, and throughout his life he was blessed with a wide, devoted, and oddly assorted circle of intimates. Dickens, as well as Browning (whose affection for Landor was largely compounded of hero-worship and gratitude), is a striking instance of Landor's capacity for creating easy and lasting relationships with men of a younger generation than himself. His disinterested encouragement of younger writers, and the complete lack of patronage in his dealings with them, were indeed among his most likeable traits. His love of children and his flair for dissolving the effects of age discrepancies did more than anything else to alleviate the rigours of his old age; among his most faithful companions at Bath were Rose Aylmer's[1] great-grandniece, and Luisina de Sodre, Ianthe's granddaughter. Even the final years of impoverished loneliness at Florence were lit by the love and companionship of the young American, Kate Field. Landor's steadfast refusal to accept the mental and spiritual sclerosis of advancing years no doubt contributed largely to his popularity with men and women many years his junior; for, despite the precocity of his early days, there remained a permanent residue of immaturity—'there is something of perpetual youth in his age', wrote a friend in the poet's sixty-sixth year. Wisdom and an inability to cope with the practical problems of social life were equally blended in Landor's make-up. His charm and intellectual vigour in middle age were such that a single encounter—as that with Coleridge or with Lamb—was enough to inspire not only respect but real affection.

[1] See note, p. 37.

13

It is interesting to trace the effect that success, coming late in life, had upon Landor. During his youth and early middle age, an ever-present sense of frustration and failure, a conviction that the world was careless of his great gifts, made him arrogant and dogmatic, indifferent to the feelings of others, often intolerably insolent; yet even during the most intransigent periods of his youth, his inviolable integrity and, when he chose to exert it, his great personal charm, could overcome all prejudices. By the time he had reached the age of fifty, however, with two volumes of the *Imaginary Conversations* published, this bogy of failure was laid; a truer appreciation of his just place upon the literary map exercised its mellowing effect and blunted the sharper prickles with which previously he had protected himself. From that time onward, although he never renounced his almost pathological independence of behaviour and opinion, new acquaintances were chiefly impressed by his courtesy and chivalrous manner.

Visits of his children to Bath, ecstatic in anticipation, were poignant and disappointing in realisation, for Arnold—to whom Landor was devoted—had grown to manhood warped by his mother's influence: a hard, pitiless, mercenary egotist. Eliza Lynn Linton leaves a vivid and endearing picture of Landor at this time: having described her first view of him, '. . . a noble looking old man, badly dressed in shabby, snuff-coloured clothes, a dirty old blue necktie, unstarched cotton shirt—with a front more like a nightgown than a shirt—and "knubbly" apple-pie boots', she goes on to write of his quick, penetrating grey-blue eyes, sweet, compelling voice, and the rare distinction of his manner. His untidiness was a reflection of the absent-mindedness which became an increasingly heavy burden in his old age. Though often as

14

trying to his friends as to himself, this was not without its humorous aspects. During the Bath period it was his habit to make an annual round of visits. Arriving one year at the house of a friend with his luggage intact, he was, nevertheless, unable to unpack his *personalia* as he had left the key behind. The following year he arrived triumphantly brandishing the key—but, alas, he had forgotten the trunk.

Landor was over sixty when he began life afresh at Bath; over eighty when he left. These twenty years saw the death of one after another of his old and trusted friends. This, perhaps the cruellest penalty of old age, was particularly painful to Landor, and the pain shows in many of his later poems. Southey died in 1843, a friendship of thirty-five years severed; but the hardest blow of all fell in 1851 with the death of Ianthe.

It was at Bath that Landor reached the peak of his considerable influence as a political thinker and caustic commentator upon the contemporary scene, his philippics earning him a wholesome respect among the place-seekers and mediocre 'great'. As the grand old man of letters, one of the most brilliant conversationalists of his day, and a political philosopher of outstanding perspicuity, Landor is only comparable with some such composite figure as Shaw-Low-Wells of the present time. His unhesitating refusal to condone by silence what he considered to be corruption in any guise was characteristically the cause of his final banishment from the land of his birth.

A paltry, rather unsavoury scandal was the climax of his years at Bath. Having permitted himself to be drawn into a quarrel between two women of his acquaintance, he quickly lost all control of his indignation: calumnies and slanders flew back and forth: it was all rather childish, but Landor committed his abusive opinions to paper, and even to print. An action for libel was brought against him, and rather than stand condemned by the letter of the law whose spirit nauseated him, he packed his belongings, and in 1858, for the second time, sailed beyond the reach of legal reprisals. The trial was held in his absence, later in the year; he was found guilty, a foregone conclusion, and £1000 costs were awarded against him. 'There was grandeur', his latest biographer remarks, 'in the serenity with which the unrepentant rebel faced exile at eighty-three, having pulled up his roots for the third time in his long life.'

So opened the tragic last act of Landor's impulsive, untidy life. His family—who had remained at the Villa Gherardesca, outside Fiesole, all these years—refused to have him on his own terms. He refused to capitulate, and moved to Florence. There, in poor lodgings in the Via Nunziatina, he spent the last years of his life; and even this haven was attained largely through the intervention of the Brownings. Landor's rebellious spirit burned steadily to the end. Almost the last thing he wrote was a scathing denunciation of his landlady's shortcomings, instinct with all the fire that had ever inspired him when confronted with real or imagined injustice.

He died, a latter-day Lear, in 1864 at the age of eighty-nine. His own qualities, as much as his failings, had crouched at the root of each successive crisis of his turbulent life. This, too, Landor recognised: 'I never did a single wise thing in the whole course of my existence, although I have written many which have been thought such.'

Why is it, then, that a man of Landor's experience and intellectual stature should, nevertheless, have failed so lamentably to insinuate himself into the mental background of the ordinary man? Many *littérateurs*, even, while praising his work, confess that they cannot read it in any quantity; there could, in such circumstances, be little hope for the common reader, who may know what he likes but who is incapable of distinguishing between what he likes and what is good.

There are perhaps three chief factors contributing to Landor's neglect. His classicism cannot alone be held responsible; for Swift, to cite only one example, captured and still holds the popular imagination. More important is the sheer force and depth of Landor's intellect. He took so much for granted, having in view the 'guests few and select'; he was a scholar and a philosopher, and this shows too starkly in his writing. He made no concessions to fools, and assumed that the reader himself would be able to supply the background, where he himself contributed the foreground, the figures and the focus. The common reader—lacking on one hand the equipment of the scholar, and on the other a sophisticated appreciation of a finely wrought and morticed prose style and the beauty of mental rigour—is untouched by the peculiar excellencies of Landor: he is puzzled, he feels lost, yawns...and agrees with Dorothy Parker's pig.

Had Landor possessed the character-creating ability of a great, or even of a competent, novelist, it might have compensated for his lack of lowbrow appeal. But this, too, was no part of his equipment. He was supremely an egoist, as his life shows over and over again: to Landor, all the world was Landor. That the world he created was of so rich a magnificence is in equal measure a tribute to his art; but his self-centredness denied it the variety that can only spring from an imaginative sympathy with other men, and an appreciation of various and even contradictory windows on to reality. Landor could not create a character that was not a projection of himself, and the result was monotony. A cold literariness, even when perfect, is not a captivating quality; and the less so when divorced from a sense of humour, in which Landor was noticeably deficient.

One must take note, also, of the disturbing blind spot in Landor's critical apparatus which permitted him to perpetrate, more especially in his poems, too-frequent horrors of bathos, flatness, lifelessness, technical bungling. And while the modern reader will stomach metrical inanities, cheapness of feeling, insincerity, tubthumpery, whimsicality, in a poem, he is usually sensitive to bathos. Again, Landor frequently wrote what was little better than doggerel. But it must be remembered that he considered his versifying as being off the record—it was his relaxation, not his business. Even so, it was doggerel with a difference, and its characteristics of terseness and astringency are the reason for the inclusion of several examples in the present collection. This critical flaw in Landor, however—and it applied more widely than to literature only—represents a considerable barrier for the modern reader.

In attempting to sum up the true position and achievement of one who has received such undeservedly shabby treatment as Landor, the danger of adopting too violently partisan an attitude is ubiquitous. And in any case, summings-up may most safely be regarded as, at best, a legal convenience. But it can at least be said that it is as foolish to accept Landor's popular reputation as it is to fly to the other extreme and proclaim him as a genius comparable with Milton—as has been done before now. Landor was no Milton; but he was a phenomenon of stranger and more sombre magnificence, more profound and moving, than his universal neglect suggests.

# THE SHORTER POEMS
## *of*
# WALTER SAVAGE LANDOR

## PAST RUIN'D ILION...

Past ruin'd Ilion Helen lives,
    Alcestis rises from the shades;
Verse calls them forth; 'tis verse that gives
    Immortal youth to mortal maids.

Soon shall Oblivion's deepening veil
    Hide all the peopled hills you see,
The gay, the proud, while lovers hail
    In distant ages you and me.

The tear for fading beauty check,
    For passing glory cease to sigh;
One form shall rise above the wreck,
    One name, Ianthe, shall not die.

Landor first met Ianthe in 1803, when he was twenty-eight. She
was the strongest and most lasting personal influence in his life,
their mutual affection growing only more deep through the
years till her death, almost half a century later.

# IRELAND

Ireland never was contented...
Say you so? you are demented.
Ireland was contented when
All could use the sword and pen,
And when Tara rose so high
That her turrets split the sky,
And about her courts were seen
Liveried Angels robed in green,
Wearing, by Saint Patrick's bounty,
Emeralds big as half a county.

# IANTHE'S TROUBLES

From you, Ianthe, little troubles pass
   Like little ripples down a sunny river;
Your pleasures spring like daisies in the grass,
   Cut down, and up again as blithe as ever.

# ON SEEING A HAIR OF LUCRETIA
# BORGIA

Borgia, thou once wert almost too august,
And high for adoration;—now thou'rt dust!
All that remains of thee these plaits infold—
Calm hair, meand'ring with pellucid gold!

A single hair from the lock preserved in the Ambrosian Library
at Milan had been stolen by Byron. This he subsequently gave
to Leigh Hunt, who in turn showed it to Landor.

# DEATH OF THE DAY

My pictures blacken in their frames
    As night comes on,
And youthful maids and wrinkled dames
    Are now all one.

Death of the day! a sterner Death
    Did worse before;
The fairest form, the sweetest breath,
    Away he bore.

'...sitting afterwards without candles for about an hour as I always do...I watched the twilight darken on my walls and my pictures vanish from before me.' Letter to Forster, 1854.

## ON HENRY KETT

'The Centaur is not fabulous', said Young.
Had Young known Kett,
He had said, 'Behold one put together wrong;
The head is horseish; but, what yet
Was never seen in man or beast,
The rest is human; or, at least,
Is Kett.'

*The Centaur is not Fabulous:* Edward Young, 1755. 'Horse' Kett was a Fellow of Trinity while Landor was an undergraduate.

## *from* 'LORD BROOK AND SIR PHILIP SIDNEY'

Night airs that make tree-shadows walk, and sheep
Washed white in the cold moonshine on grey cliffs.

## TO LESBIA

I loved you once, while you loved me;
    Altho' you flirted now and then,
It only was with two or three,
    But now you more than flirt with ten.

## A CRITIC

With much ado you fail to tell
The requisites for writing well;
But, what bad writing is, you quite
Have proved by every line you write.

## ULYSSES-LIKE HAD MYRRHA KNOWN...

Ulysses-like had Myrrha known,
Aye, many a man in many a town:
At last she swore that she would be
Constant to one alone, to me.
She fails a trifle: I reprove:
Myrrha no longer swears her love;
One falsehood honest Myrrha spares,
And argues better than she swears.
'Look now', says she, 'o'er these fair plains,
What find you there that long remains?
The rocks upon yon ugly hill
Are hard and cold and changeless stil.'

## VERSES WHY BURNT

How many verses have I thrown
Into the fire because the one
Peculiar word, the wanted most,
Was irrecoverably lost.

## SWIFT ON POPE

### (IMAGINARY)

Pope, tho' his letters are so civil,
Wishes me fairly at the devil;
A little dentifrice and soap
Is all the harm I wish poor Pope.


## THERE IS A TIME...

There is a time when the romance of life
Should be shut up, and closed with double clasp:
Better that this be done before the dust
That none can blow away falls into it.


## PLAYS

Alas, how soon the hours are over,
Counted us out to play the lover!
And how much narrower is the stage,
Allotted us to play the sage!
But when we play the fool, how wide
The theatre expands; beside,
How long the audience sits before us!
How many prompters! what a chorus!


## ON THE SMOOTH BROW...

On the smooth brow and clustering hair
    Myrtle and rose! your wreath combine;
The duller olive I would wear,
    Its constancy, its peace, be mine.

## LINES TO A DRAGON FLY

Life (priest and poet say) is but a dream;
   I wish no happier one than to be laid
   Beneath some cool syringa's scented shade
Or wavy willow, by the running stream,
   Brimful of Moral, where the Dragon Fly
   Wanders as careless and content as I.

Thanks for this fancy, insect king,
Of purple crest and filmy wing,
Who with indifference givest up
The water-lily's golden cup,
To come again and overlook
What I am writing in my book.
Believe me, most who read the line
Will read with hornier eyes than thine;
And yet their souls shall live for ever,
And thine drop dead into the river!
God pardon them, O insect king,
Who fancy so unjust a thing!

## THE GEORGES

George the First was always reckoned
Vile, but viler George the Second;
And what mortal ever heard
Any good of George the Third?
When from earth the Fourth descended
(God be praised!) the Georges ended.

## WHY, WHY REPINE...?

Why, why repine, my pensive friend,
　　At pleasures slipt away?
Some the stern Fates will never lend,
　　And all refuse to stay.

I see the rainbow in the sky,
　　The dew upon the grass,
I see them, and I ask not why
　　They glimmer or they pass.

With folded arms I linger not
　　To call them back; 'twere vain;
In this, or in some other spot,
　　I know they'll shine again.


## AN ANGEL FROM HIS PARADISE...

An angel from his Paradise drove Adam;
From mine a devil drove me—Thank you, Madam.


## WISE AND UNWISE

To love and to be loved the wise would give
All that for which alone the unwise strive.


## THERE ARE SWEET FLOWERS...

There are sweet flowers that only blow by night,
And sweet tears are there that avoid the light;
No mortal sees them after day is born,
They, like the dew, drop trembling from their thorn.

## from 'IZAAC WALTON, COTTON, AND WILLIAM OLDWAYS'

In my bosom I would rather
Daffodils and kingcups gather,
Than have fifty sighing souls,
False as cats and dull as owls.

## VARIOUS THE ROADS...

Various the roads of life; in one
    All terminate, one lonely way.
We go; and 'Is he gone?'
    Is all our best friends say.

## RELIEF AT THE CRIMEA

Flannel, and potted meat, and rum,
Before the dogdays will have come
In Ellesmere's expected yacht...
I know but one event like that.
Here is the story...I remember
About the middle of December
Ice fringed the Arno, crisp and clear,
And upon shallow pools might bear.
A gentleman from Tipperary,
Alert as he is wise and wary,
Wrote home for skates: one fine May morn
The skates he wrote for reach Leghorn.

Lord Ellesmere's relief yacht arrived at the Crimea in
February 1855.

## ACCORDING TO ETERNAL LAWS...

According to eternal laws
('Tis useless to inquire the cause)
The gates of fame and of the grave
Stand under the same architrave,
So I would rather some time yet
Play on with you, my little pet!

## IMPROMPTU

But he is foolish who supposes
Dogs are ill that have hot noses.

## WITH AN ALBUM

I know not whether I am proud,
But this I know, I hate the crowd:
Therefore pray let me disengage
My verses from the motley page,
Where others far more sure to please
Pour out their choral song with ease.
And yet perhaps, if some should tire
With too much froth or too much fire,
There is an ear that may incline
Even to words so dull as mine.

## THE CRIMEAN HEROES

Hail, ye indomitable heroes, hail!
Despite of all your generals ye prevail.

## MUSIC

Interminable undulating weeds
Cover sharp rocks along the sea's abyss;
Thou buoyant music waves about the breast
And lifts it up from what lies dark below.


## TELL ME NOT THINGS PAST
## ALL BELIEF...

Tell me not things past all belief;
One truth in you I prove;
The flame of anger, bright and brief,
Sharpens the barb of Love.


## A PARAPHRASE ON JOB

'*A Paraphrase on Job*' we see
By Young: it loads the shelf:
He who can read one half must be
Patient as Job himself.

*A Paraphrase on the Book of Job:* Edward Young, 1719.


## LAST WORDS

Pretty Anne Boleyn made a joke
On her thin neck, just when the stroke
That was to sever it was nigh,
And show'd how innocence should die.
The wittier and the wiser More
With equal pace had gone before.
Earlier in Athens died the sage

Who's death o'er Plato's puzzling page
Sheds its best light: well matcht with these
Was shrewd and sturdy Socrates.
He laught not at the gods aloud,
For that would irritate the crowd;
But, not to die in debt, he said,
'Let Æsculapius have his fee
For radically curing me.
A gamecock he deserves at least
So catch and take one to his priest.'

## CARLYLE

Strike with Thor's hammer, strike agen
The skulking heads of half-form'd men,
And every northern God shall smile
Upon thy well-aim'd blow, Carlyle!

## WHAT NEWS

Here, ever since you went abroad,
    If there be change, no change I see,
I only walk our wonted road,
    The road is only walkt by me.

Yes; I forgot; a change there is;
    Was it of *that* you bade me tell?
I catch at times, at times I miss
    The sight, the tone, I know so well.

Only two months since you stood here!
    Two shortest months! then tell me why
Voices are harsher than they were,
    And tears are longer ere they dry.

## FRIENDS

The heaviest curse that can on mortal fall
Is 'who has friends may he outlive them all!'
This malediction has awaited me
Who had so many...I could once count three.

## MILITARY MERIT REWARDED

Worth is rewarded, even here,
    With praises; nor is *this* all:
Havelock wins fivescore pounds a year,
    And Guyon...a dismissal.

But Napier, who on many a day
    Perform'd the foremost part,
And fill'd the murderers with dismay...
    He won...a broken heart.

General Sir Charles Napier, died 1853. His brother, the historian
of the Peninsular War, was also an intimate friend of Landor.

## YOU SMILED, YOU SPOKE...

You smiled, you spoke, and I believed,
By every word and smile deceived.
Another man would hope no more;
Nor hope I what I hoped before;
But let not this last wish be vain;
Deceive, deceive me once again!

## BYRON

There is a restless mortal who
Feeds on himself, and eats for two.
Heartburn all day and night he feels
And never tries to walk but reels.

Boy! on the table set the taper
And bring your lucifer; this paper
I must without delay set fire on
Or folks may fancy I mean Byron.
Be petty larcenies forgiven,
The fire he stole was not from heaven.

Landor allowed his dislike of Byron's way of life to cloud his appreciation both of Byron's work and of the more estimable facets of his character. On hearing of the manner of his death, however, Landor made a full recantation.

## TWENTY YEARS HENCE...

Twenty years hence my eyes may grow
If not quite dim, yet rather so,
Still yours from others they shall know
    Twenty years hence.
Twenty years hence tho' it may hap
That I be call'd to take a nap
In a cool cell where thunder-clap
    Was never heard.
There breathe but o'er my arch of grass
A not too sadly sigh'd *Alas*,
And I shall catch, ere you can pass,
    That winged word.

## THE GOOD-NATURED FRIEND

Some if they're forced to tell the truth
Tell it you with a sad, wry mouth,
And make it plainly understood
Such never was their natural food.

# DIALOGUE

*Old man:*     What wouldst thou say,
Autumnal day,
Clothed in a mist akin to rain?

*Dark day:*     Thus I appear,
Because next year,
Perhaps we may not meet again.

# ON A WEDDING

Blest idiot! with thy vicarage and thy wife,
    Why dost thou chuckle so? come prythee say?
Then I will tell thee—thou hast gain'd for life,
    To be awake all night, asleep all day.

# WELL I REMEMBER HOW
# YOU SMILED...

Well I remember how you smiled
    To see me write your name upon
The soft sea-sand...'*Oh! what a child!*
    *You think you're writing upon stone!*'
I have since written what no tide
    Shall ever wash away, what men
Unborn shall read o'er ocean wide
    And find Ianthe's name agen.

## WHY SHOULD THE SCRIBBLERS
## DISCOMPOSE...?

Why should the scribblers discompose
Our temper? would we look like those?
There are some curs in every street
Who snarl and snap at all they meet:
The taller mastif deems it aptest
To lift a leg and play the baptist.


## JOY IS THE BLOSSOM...

Joy is the blossom, sorrow is the fruit,
Of human life; and worms are at the root.


## VERY TRUE, THE LINNETS SING...

Very true, the linnets sing
Sweetest in the leaves of spring:
You have found in all these leaves
That which changes and deceives,
And, to pine by sun or star,
Left them, false ones as they are.
But there be who walk beside
Autumn's, till they all have died,
And who lend a patient ear
To low notes from branches sere.


## GIRL AND DIOGENES

'Men call you *dog*: now tell me why',
A little girl said: in reply
Diogenes said, smiling at her,
'My child! how wickedly men flatter!'

## RETIRE, AND TIMELY, FROM
## THE WORLD...

Retire, and timely, from the world, if ever
    Thou hopest tranquil days;
Its gaudy jewels from thy bosom sever,
    Despise its pomp and praise.
The purest star that looks into the stream
    Its slightest ripple shakes,
And Peace, where'er its fiercer splendours gleam,
    Her brooding nest forsakes.
The quiet planets roll with even motion
    In the still skies alone;
O'er ocean they dance joyously, but ocean
    They find no rest upon.


## TO LYSIS

### (FROM 'PERICLES AND ASPASIA')

A curse upon the king of old
  Who would have kidnapt all the Muses!
Whether to barter them for gold
  Or keep them for his proper uses.

Lysis! aware he meant them ill,
  Birds they became, and flew away...
Thy Muse alone continues still
  A titmouse to this very day.


## MARCH 24

Sharp crocus wakes the froward year;
In their old haunts birds reappear;
From yonder elm, yet black with rain,
The cushat looks deep down for grain

34

Thrown on the gravel-walk; here comes
The redbreast to the sill for crumbs.
Fly off! fly off! I cannot wait
To welcome ye, as she of late.
The earliest of my friends is gone.
Alas! almost my only one!
The few as dear, long wafted o'er,
Await me on a sunnier shore.


## *from* 'SOUTHEY AND PORSON'

Dank, limber verses, stuft with lakeside sedges,
And propt with rotten stakes from broken hedges.

Porson is speaking of some verses by Wordsworth.


## A FOREN RULER

He says, *My reign is peace,* so slays
    A thousand in the dead of night.
*Are you all happy now?* he says,
    And those he leaves behind cry *quite.*
He swears he will have no contention,
    And sets all nations by the ears;
He shouts aloud, *No intervention!*
    Invades, and drowns them all in tears.


## BLYTHE BELL, THAT CALLS TO
## BRIDAL HALLS...

Blythe bell, that calls to bridal halls,
    Tolls deep a darker day;
The very shower that feeds the flower
    Weeps also its decay.

## EPIGRAM

Know ye the land where from its acrid root
The sweet nepenthè rears her ripen'd fruit,
Which whoso tastes forgets his house and home?
Ye know it not: come on then; come to Rome.
Behold upon their knees with cord and scourge
Men, full-grown men, pale puffy phantasts urge!
Holiness lies with them in fish and frogs,
Mid squealing eunuchs and mid sculptured logs,
Mid gaudy dresses changed for every scene,
And mumbled prayers in unknown tongue between.
These wrongs imposed on them they call their rights!
For these the poor man toils, the brave man fights!
Exclaiming 'Saints above! your triumphs o'er,
Shall roasted Ridleys crown the feast no more?
Shall all our candles gutter into gloom,
And faith sit still, or only sweep the room?'


## BOURBONS

Isabella spits at Spain,
    Bomba strips and scourges Naples:
Are there not then where they reign
    Rotten eggs or rotten apples?

Halters, gibbets, axes, blocks!
    Your old textbook ye forget:
Treadmills, pillories, humbler stocks!
    Ye perform your duties yet.

Men have often heard the thunder
    Roll at random; where, O where
Rolls it now?  I smell it under
    That fat priest in that foul chair.

Never was there poet wanting
    Where the lapdog licks the throne;
Lauds and hymns we hear them chanting,
    Shame if I were mute alone!

Let me then your deeds rehearse,
    Gem of kings and flower of queens!
Tho' I may but trail a verse
    Languider than Lamartine's.

## MILTON

Will mortals never know each other's station
Without the herald?  O abomination!
Milton, even Milton, rankt with living men!
Over the highest Alps of mind he marches,
And far below him spring the baseless arches
Of Iris, coloring dimly lake and fen.

## PROMISE

I may not add to youth's brief days
    Nor bid the fleeting hours stand still;
No, Rose; but I can waft your praise
    To distant ages, and I will.
Forgotten be my name if yours
In its fresh purity endures.

Landor met Rose Aylmer at Swansea in 1796, and, ever sus-
ceptible, fell in love with her.  Four years later she died of
cholera in India.

## ADVICE

A scholar was about to marry,
His friend said, 'Ere thou dost, be wary.
So wise art thou that I forsee
A wife will make a fool of thee.
Foolishest of all fools are those
Wise men led daily by the nose.
It hardly seems a woman's while
The fond half-witted to beguile:
And yet I must confess, my friend,
Sometimes they do so condescend.'


## MILD IS THE PARTING YEAR...

Mild is the parting year, and sweet
  The odour of the falling spray;
Life passes on more rudely fleet,
  And balmless is its closing day.

I wait its close, I court its gloom,
  But mourn that never there must fall
Or on my breast or on my tomb
  The tear that would have soothed it all.


## from 'IZAAC WALTON, COTTON, AND WILLIAM OLDWAYS'

Juno was proud, Minerva stern,
Venus would rather toy than learn.
What fault is there in Margaret Hayes?
Her high disdain and pointed stayes.

## PROUD WORD YOU NEVER SPOKE...

Proud word you never spoke, but you will speak
    Four not exempt from pride some future day.
Resting on one white hand a warm wet cheek
    Over my open volume you will say,
    'This man loved *me*!' then rise and trip away.

## GIBBON

Gibbon has planted laurels long to bloom
Above the ruins of sepulchral Rome.
He sang no dirge, but mused upon the land
Where Freedom took his solitary stand.
To him Thucydides and Livius bow,
And Superstition veils her wrinkled brow.

## PORTRAIT

Thy skin is like an unwasht carrot's,
Thy tongue is blacker than a parrot's,
Thy teeth are crooked, but belong
Inherently to such a tongue.

This 'Portrait' is one of the libellous poems which led to
Landor's final banishment from England. It is included here for
its biographical rather than its poetic interest.

## IGNORANCE OF BOTANY

I hardly know one flower that grows
    On my small garden plot;
Perhaps I may have seen a *Rose*
    And said, *Forget-me-not.*

## WORDSWORTH HAS WELL DESERVED
## OF LATE...

Wordsworth has well deserved of late
A very pretty doctorate!
O Dons! I would desire no more
Could you make *me* a bachelor.


## ACROSS, UP, DOWN, OUR
## FORTUNES GO...

Across, up, down, our fortunes go,
Like particles of feathery snow,
Never so certain or so sound
As when they're fallen to the ground.


## TRANSLATION OF IAMBI 51

Left-handed is that liberality, Russell,
Which places in office and seats on one trussel
   The wise and the foolish, as you have just done.
The fleet of old England to him you confide
Who never had mounted a pinnace's side,
   To whom mast and foresail and rudder are one.

True! true! 'Tis according to court-regulation
That all the first honours and trusts of the nation
   Be theirs, and theirs only, whom Plutus has blest:
Yet here is an Auckland, whom lads of the north
Are used to call Lackland, so little in worth
   A furlong is more than he ever possest.

Thus talk and thus reason the vulgar, but we
No harm, where no pride is, in poverty see.
    Were he lying and scratching his ribs in the street
It is not unlikely that we should be willing
To give him a penny, to give him a shilling,
    But never, good Johnny, to give him a fleet.

A free rendering of the poem 'Ad I. Russellum' which was included in the 1847 volume, *Poemata, etc.* The Earl of Auckland
was First Lord of the Admiralty in Lord John Russell's ministry
of 1846.


## SHAKESPEARE IN ITALY

Beyond our shores, past Alps and Appennines,
    Shakespeare, from heaven came thy creative breath,
Mid citron groves and over-arching vines
    Thy genius wept at Desdemona's death.
In the proud sire thou badest anger cease
And Juliet by her Romeo sleep in peace;
Then rose thy voice above the stormy sea,
And Ariel flew from Prospero to thee.


## REPLY TO AN INVITATION

*Will you come to the bower I have shaded for you?*
*Our couch shall be roses all spangled with dew.*
Tommy Moore, Tommy Moore, I'll be hang'd if I do,
It would give me a cough, and a rheumatise too.
The girl who is prudent, I take it would rather
Repose (tho' alone) upon horsehair or feather.
Poor Peggy O'Corcoran listened to some
Who sang in her ear, *Will you come? Will you come?*
She swells and she squaddles...so what I suppose is
She must have been lying one day upon roses.

# ON ENGLISH HEXAMETERS

Porson was askt what he thought of hexameters written in
  English:
'Show me', said he, 'any five in continuance true to the
  meter,
Five where a dactyl has felt no long syllable puncht thro' his
  midrif,
Where not a trochee or pyrric has stood on one leg at the
  entrance
Like a grey fatherly crane keeping watch on the marsh at
  Cayster.
Zounds! how they hop, skip, and jump! Old Homer, up-
  lifting his eyebrows,
Cries to the somnolent Gods...O ye blessed who dwell
  on Olympos!
What have I done in old-age? have I ever complain'd of my
  blindness?
Ye in your wisdom may deem that a poet sings only the
  better
(Some little birds do) for *that*; but why are my ears to be
  batter'd
Flat to my head as a mole's or a fish's, if fishes have any?
Why do barbarians rush with a fury so headstrong against
  me?
Have they no poet at home they can safely and readily
  waylay?'
 Then said a youth in his gown, 'I do humbly beg pardon,
  Professor,
But are you certain that you, to whom all the wide Hellas is
  open,
Could make Homer, who spoke many dialects with many
  nations,
Speak, as we now have attempted to teach him, our pure
  Anglo-saxon?'

Then the Professor, 'I wager a dozen of hock or of claret,
Standing on only one foot I can throw off more verses and
      better
Than the unlucky, that limp and halt and have "*no foot to
      stand on*".'
''Pon my word, as I live!' said a younger, 'I really think he
      has done it,
Every soul of us here, by a score of hexameters, quizzing.'

Porson: the eminent Greek scholar (1759–1808) and focal point
of a catholic and brilliant circle of writers and intellectuals.


## 'I'M HALF IN LOVE'...

'I'm half in love', he who with smiles hath said
    In love will never be.
Who'er, 'I'm not in love', and shakes his head,
    In love too sure is he.


## TO PETER THE FISHERMAN

Thou hast been ever active, Peter,
    And netted loads on loads of fish;
Could we but get them somewhat sweeter
    'Twere well...alas, how vain the wish!
We must remember that they come
    Close-hamper'd all the way through Rome.

## ROSE AYLMER

Ah what avails the sceptred race,
　　Ah what the form divine!
What every virtue, every grace!
　　Rose Aylmer, all were thine.
Rose Aylmer, whom these wakeful eyes
　　May weep, but never see,
A night of memories and sighs
　　I consecrate to thee.

Written in 1800, on hearing of Rose Aylmer's death.


## THE DUKE OF YORK'S STATUE

Enduring is the bust of bronze,
And thine, O flower of George's sons,
Stands high above all laws and duns.

As honest men as ever cart
Convey'd to Tyburn took thy part
And raised thee up to where thou art.


## THE PIGEON-FANCIER

Some are fanciers in religions,
Some (the wiser they) in pigeons.
I confess it, I prefer
Much the pigeon-fancier.
For I never knew him spill
Pigeon's blood, nor threaten ill,
Whether hell's or kitchen's flame...
Can those others say the same?
Fools! to fancy loads of faggot
Are required to cook a maggot!

## WRITTEN IN 1793

'Tell me what means that sigh', Ione said,
When on her shoulder I reclined my head;
And I could only tell her that it meant
The sigh that swells the bosom with content.

Ione was Landor's name for Nancy Jones, a Welsh precursor
of the Irish Ianthe, whom he met at Tenby. Evidence has
recently come to light which may indicate that Ione presented
Landor with a daughter, who, however, died in early infancy.


## SENT WITH POEMS

Little volume, warm with wishes,
    Fear not brows that never frown!
After Byron's peppery dishes
    Matho's mild skim-milk goes down.

Change she wants not, self-concenter'd,
    She whom Attic graces please,
She whose Genius never enter'd
    Literature's gin-palaces.


## SHELLEY AND KEATS, ON
## EARTH UNKNOWN...

Shelley and Keats, on earth unknown
One to the other, now are gone
Where only such pure Spirits meet
And sing before them words as sweet.

## I SAW UPON HIS PULPIT-PERCH...

I saw upon his pulpit-perch
A well-fed gamecock of the church
Spread out his plumes, and heard him crow
To his lean pullets croucht below.
'Wretches! ye raise your throats to men
Who pry into your father's pen;
Look at your betters, do as they do,
And be content to chant a *credo*.'


## SQUIBS, CRACKERS, SERPENTS...

Squibs, crackers, serpents, rockets, Bengal lights,
Lead thousands running to the Dardanelles,
Where girls by sackfuls bubble thro' the wave;
I, leaving good old Homer, not o'erlong,
Enjoy the merriment of Chaucer's tales
Or louder glee of the large-hearted Burns,
And then partaking Southey's wholesome fare,
Plenteous, and savoury, without spice, I turn,
To my own sofa, where incontinent
Wordsworth's low coo brings over me sound sleep.


## QUARREL

*Man:*  Work on marble shall not be,
Lady fair! the work for me:
For which reason you and I
May together say *good-bye*.

*Lady:*  Say of marble what you will,
Work on sand is vainer still:
For which reason I and you
Very wisely say *adieu*.

46

## REMAIN, AH NOT IN YOUTH ALONE...

Remain, ah not in youth alone,
   Tho' youth, where you are, long will stay,
But when my summer days are gone,
   And my autumnal haste away.

*'Can I be always by your side?'*
   No; but the hours you can, you must,
Nor rise at Death's approaching stride,
   Nor go when dust is gone to dust.


## THE CONTRITE PRIEST

Incline, O Mary, from thy throne
To hear a contrite sinner own
His manifold and grievous sins,
Thick as the serried ranks of pins,
But first (for time is precious) hear
What the black score in part may clear.
   I always ate (for 'twas thy wish,
On Fridays we should dine on fish)
Turbot or lamprey or whate'er
The cook thought proper to prepare;
Ay, I have been constrain'd to stoop
To creeping things, and sigh o'er soup
Founded on oysters, taught to swim
For the first time in beardless trim.
   Ah, lady! couldst thou only know
The anguish of my heart and toe!
Help! tis impossible without
Thy help to keep at bay the gout.

# EPIGRAM

There are two miseries in human life;
To live without a friend, and with a wife.


## LADY HOLLAND

Our steam navigation
And blood's circulation
Are wonders in Science and Art.
Far greater his *nous*
The physician's who shows
In Holland's old spouse
A heart! an affection of heart.

'These... came into my head on hearing Talfourd say that Lady
Holland had an affection of the heart.' Letter to Lady Blessington,
1836.


## THE SOLAR MICROSCOPE

You want a powerful lens to see
What animalcules those may be,
Which float about the smallest drop
Of water, and which never stop,
Pursuing each that goes before,
And rolling in unrest for more.

Poets! a watery world is ours,
Where each floats after, each devours,
Its little unsubstantial prey...
Strange animalcules...we and they!

## ONE TOOTH HAS MUMMIUS...

One tooth has Mummius; but in sooth
No man has such another tooth:
Such a prodigious tooth would do
To moor the bark of Charon to,
Or better than the Sinai stone,
To grave the Ten Commandments on.

'Mummius' is replaced by 'Wordsworth' in one reprint.
Landor, while admiring much of Wordsworth's work, could not
endure him as a man. One of the most crushing summings-up
of Wordsworth ever uttered came from Landor: 'Wordsworth
is a strange mixture of sheep and wolf, with one eye on a daffodil
and the other on a canal-share.' In another of the *Imaginary
Conversations*, Landor says, 'In Wordsworth's poetry there is
as much of prose as there is of poetry in the prose of Milton.
But prose on certain occasions can bear a great deal of poetry:
on the other hand, poetry sinks and swoons under a moderate
weight of prose.'

## TOO MINDFUL OF THE FAULT
## IN EVE...

Too mindful of the fault in Eve,
You ladies never will believe,
Else I would venture now to say
I love you quite as well this day
As when fire ran along my veins
From your bright eyes, and joys and pains
Each other's swelling waves pursued,
And when the wooer too was wooed.

## ON THE DOG-STAR

I hold it unlawful
To question the awful
Appointments of Heaven, or hazard a doubt;
But needs I must say,
Heaven's Dog had his day,
And Pomero beats the said Dog out and out.

Pomero was a white Pomeranian sent to Landor by his daughter
in 1844. For twelve years the dignified figure of Landor, and
the prancing, volatile Pomero were one of the familiar sights of
Bath.

## TO A YOUNG POET

The camel at the city-gate
Bends his flat head, and there must wait.
Thin in the desert is the palm,
And pierced the thorn to give its balm.
The Land of Promise thou shalt see,
I swear it, by myself and thee;
Rise, cheer thee up, and look round,
All earth is not for deer and hound;
Worms revel in the slime of kings,
But perish where the laurel springs.

## GOVERNORS OF INDIA

Auckland, Dalhousie, Canning! shall we ever
Again see three such rulers? three so clever
At shattering the foundations of a state
And hastening on the heavy step of Fate.

## I CAN NOT TELL...

I can not tell, not I, why she
Awhile so gracious, now should be
So grave: I can not tell you why
The violet hangs its head awry.
It shall be cull'd, it shall be worn,
In spite of every sign of scorn,
Dark look, and overhanging thorn.


## IF THE DEVIL...

If the Devil, a mighty old omnibus driver
Saw an omnibus driving down-hill to the river
And saved any couple to share his own cab
I do really think 'twould be Gabell and Gabb.

Gabell and Gabb were the two Abergavenny lawyers whose
unscrupulous mishandling of Landor's interests during the in-
volved Llanthony proceedings drove him to that pitch of
frustrated rage at which he washed his hands for ever of Llanthony, the fortune he had spent on it, and the Welsh.


## BASED ON A FRAGMENT
## BY SAPPHO

Mother, I cannot mind my wheel;
   My fingers ache, my lips are dry:
Oh! if you felt the pain I feel!
   But Oh, who ever felt as I?

No longer could I doubt him true;
   All other men may use deceit:
He always said my eyes were blue,
   And often swore my lips were sweet.

## REFLECTION FROM SEA AND SKY

When I gaze upon the sky
And the sea below, I cry,
Thus be poetry and love,
Deep beneath and bright above.

## THE MAID'S LAMENT

I loved him not; and yet, now he is gone,
    I feel I am alone.
I check'd him while he spoke; yet, could he speak,
    Alas! I would not check.
For reasons not to love him once I sought,
    And wearied all my thought
To vex myself and him: I now would give
    My love could he but live
Who lately lived for me, and, when he found
    'Twas vain, in holy ground
He hid his face amid the shades of death!
    I waste for him my breath
Who wasted his for me! but mine returns,
    And this lorn bosom burns
With stifling heat, heaving it up in sleep,
    And waking me to weep
Tears that had melted his soft heart: for years
    Wept he as bitter tears!
*Merciful God!* such was his latest prayer,
    *These may she never share!*
Quieter is his breath, his breast more cold,
    Than daisies in the mould,
Where children spell, athwart the churchyard gate,
    His name and life's brief date.
Pray for him, gentle souls, whoe'er you be,
    And, oh! pray too for me!

## THE LEAVES ARE FALLING...

The leaves are falling; so am I;
The few late flowers have moisture in the eye;
 So have I too.
Scarcely on any bough is heard
Joyous, or even unjoyous, bird
 The whole wood through.

Winter may come: he brings but nigher
His circle (yearly narrowing) to the fire
 Where old friends meet:
Let him; now heaven is overcast,
And spring and summer both are past,
 And all things sweet.


## A BACK-BITER

If thou wert only foul and frowsy,
If only itchy, only lousy,
Bold men might take thy hand, Dalhousie!

Thou art a prudent chiel, my lord,
And in thy little heart are stored
Lies stampt and mill'd, a precious hoard!

If thou hadst only run away
While Napier kept our foes at bay,
None would have cried, '*Come back! stay, stay!*'

Many like thee are not o'er-brave,
Like thee their bacon they would save,
But ne'er besmirch a veteran's grave.

Sir James Ramsay, first Marquis of Dalhousie (1812–60):
Governor-General of India, 1847–57, where he pressed forward
a policy of imperialist annexation.

## O IMMORTALITY OF FAME!...

O immortality of fame!
What art thou? even Shakespeare's name
Reaches not Shakespeare in his grave.
The wise, the virtuous, and the brave,
Resume ere long their common clay,
And worms are longer lived than they.
At last some gilded letters show
What those were call'd who lie below.

## RIVAL LAWYERS

Two rival lawyers, Gabb and Gabell,
Make Abergany comfortable.
To Welshmen stiff and heady quarrels
Are needful as their *cwrw*-barrels;
Of both they quaff, sup after sup,
Until they fairly are laid up.

## ON AGESILAO MILANO

Even the brave abase the head
To lick the dust that tyrants tread;
Not thus Milano: he alone
Would bow to Justice on the throne.
To wear a crown of thorns he trod
A flinty path, and slept with God.

Landor, a perfervid advocate of tyrannicide, felt strongly for
Milano, who in 1856 was court-martialled and hanged for
making an attack with his bayonet upon King Ferdinand II
during a military review at Naples.

## PEOPLE AND PATRIOTS

People like best the patriots who betray 'em;
They trusted Russell and they trusted Graham;
Past folly's last extreme they now are gone,
And pant, and halt, and cling to Palmerston.

## A POET'S LEGACY

Above all gifts we most should prize
The wisdom that makes others wise:
To others when ourselves are dust
We leave behind this sacred trust.

We may not know, when we are gone,
The good we shall on earth have done;
Enough in going is the thought
For once we acted as we ought.

## TO ROSE

If by my death I win a tear,
   O Rose, why should I linger here?
If my departure cost you two,
   Alas! I shall be loth to go.

## ILL SUCCESS OF SAINT PETER

Saint Peter could fish up
No shark of a bishop
In the waters of far Galilee,
So he rigs a new skiff
And is wondering if
He can find one in Exeter See.

Dr Philpotts became Bishop of Exeter in 1831.

## WHO IS SAFE?

Men always hate
The man that's great,
Nor cease to fall
On him that's small.

## THE DEAN'S TALE

Driven from manse and kaleyard when
The kirk had lost her stoutest men,
Mas Thomas hotly was pursued
By Philistines athirst for blood.
In Scotland there is scarcely brake
Sufficient to conceal a snake.
The Lady Cherrytree was one
Whom Mas could more relie upon,
She was so kindly and so staid
And kept the sabbath where he pray'd.
At nightfall, then he took the road
Where that good lady's mansion stood.
The troopers presently drew near,
But he had enter'd dumb with fear.
*Hide me!* were the first words he spake,
*O hide me quick for Jesu's sake!*
She caught him by the arm and led
Hurriedly to her daughter's bed.
There was no other place so sure
And he was holy, she was pure.
The girl slept soundly; he crept in
Under her, for they both were thin.
She turn'd a little, but no light
Guided her eyes.

*All right, all right,*
Whispered the mother, *lie thee still*;
*Trust in the Lord and fear no ill.*
*Let thy two knees be wide and bent,*
Said she and saw it done, then went.

The troop soon entered and they heard
A drowsy breath, but saw no beard.
While they were searching what did he?
He grafted a young Cherry tree.

Charles, when the tale was told, cried 'Zounds!
*I'm glad the fox escaped the hounds,*
*The scent was lost, the chace was over*
Renard was fairly run to cover.
Bring us the saintly rogue, he ought
To find a welcome at our court.
Up in the oak I could not do
What Mas did, Rochester, could you?'

This poem, never published during Landor's lifetime, was discovered in his desk after his death. The incident on which it is based is recounted in Captain Creichton's *Memoirs*, 1731.

## *from* MOSCHUS, IDYL III

Ah! when the mallow in the croft dies down,
Or the pale parsley or the crisped anise,
Again they grow, another year they flourish;
But we, the great, the valiant, and the wise,
Once covered over in the hollow earth,
Sleep a long, dreamless, unawakening sleep.

## IS IT NOT BETTER AT AN
## EARLY HOUR...?

Is it not better at an early hour
  In its calm cell to rest the weary head,
While birds are singing and while blooms the bower,
  Than sit the fire out and go starv'd to bed?


## IF YOU NO LONGER LOVE ME... .

    If you no longer love me,
      To friendship why pretend?
    Unworthy was the lover,
      Unworthy be the friend.
    I know there is another
      Of late prefer'd to me:

    Recover'd is my freedom,
      And you again are free.
    I've seen the bird that summer
      Deluded from her spray
    Return again in winter
      And grieve she flew away.


## WILLIAM GIFFORD

Clap, clap the double nightcap on!
  Gifford will read you his amours...
Lazy as Scheld and cold as Don...
  Kneel, and thank Heaven they are not yours.

William Gifford (1756–1826): first editor of the *Quarterly Review*.

## SEPARATION

There is a mountain and a wood between us,
Where the lone shepherd and late bird have seen us
Morning and noon and even-tide repass.
Between us now the mountain and the wood
Seem standing darker than last year they stood,
And say we must not cross, alas! alas!

## ON THE HEIGHTS

The cattle in the common field
    Toss their flat heads in vain,
And snort and stamp; weak creatures yield
    And turn back home again.

My mansion stands beyond it, high
    Above where rushes grow;
Its hedge of laurel dares defy
    The heavy-hooft below.

## CREDO

I do believe a drop of water
May save us from the fire herea'ter.
I do believe a crumb of bread,
O'er which the priest his prayer hath said,
May be the richest flesh and blood...
I would believe too, if I could,
*Pius's* word is worth a crumb
Or drop; but here awe strikes me dumb.

## ON LAW

What thousands, Law, thy handywork deplore!
Thou hangest many, but thou starvest more.

## IDLE WORDS

They say that every idle word
Is numbered by the Omniscient Lord.
O Parliament! 'tis well that He
Endureth for Eternity,
And that a thousand Angels wait
To write them at thy inner gate.


## THE DAY RETURNS...

The day returns, my natal day,
  Borne on the storm and pale with snow,
And seems to ask me why I stay,
  Stricken by Time and bowed by Woe.

Many were once the friends who came
  To wish me joy; and there are some
Who wish it now; but not the same;
  They are whence friend can never come;

Nor are they you my love watcht o'er
  Cradled in innocence and sleep;
You smile into my eyes no more,
  Nor see the bitter tears they weep.


## ESPOUSALS OF H.M. OF PORTUGAL

Youngster of Coburg! thou hast found a throne
Easy to mount, and easier to slip down:
But, in the name of wonder! who beside
Of mortal men could mount thy royal bride?
So vast an enterprize requires the force
And ladder too that scaled the Trojan horse,

In whose rank orifice some hundreds hid
Themselves and arms, and down the rampire slid.
Thou hast achieved a mightier deed and bolder,
And hast not dislocated hip or shoulder.

Prince Ferdinand Augustus of Saxe-Coburg and Gotha married
Queen Maria II da Gloria, of Braganza, in 1836.

## INVITATION

If there be any who would rather
Short thyme from steep Hymettus gather,
Than thro' Hyrcanian forests trudge
In heavy boots, knee-deep in sludge,
Come, here is room enough for you,
There will be round about but few.

## DOCTOR'D BY BACON AND
## MONTAIGNE...

Doctor'd by Bacon and Montaigne
My eyebrows may sprout forth again,
Worne by hard rubbing to make out
Plato's interminable doubt.
Around him were some clever folks
Until they stumbled into jokes;
Incontinent I quitted these
To stroll with Aristophanes.
I'd rather sup on cold potato,
Than on a salmi cookt by Plato,
Who, always nice but never hearty,
Says Homer shall not join the party.

## THE MATRON

Become a matron, grave and sage,
You, reprehending every page
That pleas'd you not long since, seem now
To ask from under frowning brow,
'Ha! what audacity hath placed
This volume in a hand so chaste?
A volume where fictitious names
Cover, not hide, forbidden flames.'
  Be merciful! and let him pass;
He is no longer what he was:
He wrote as poets wrote before,
And loved like them...but rather more.


## GEORGE THE THIRD'S STATUE

Altho' against thee, George the Third!
I threw sometimes a scornful word,
Against thy nape I did not nail
Characteristical pig-tail.
What is thy genus none can doubt
Who looks but at thy brow and snout.

Wyatt's statue of George III, now in Pall Mall, was erected in
1837.


## MISTS

Why are there mists and clouds to-day?
It is that Rose is far away:
The sun refuses to arise,
And will not shine but from her eyes.

## CROKER

Disposer of our fleet is Croker,
He should have been at most a stoker.

J. W. Croker: for over twenty years Secretary to the Admiralty,
resigned in 1830.

## WEAK MINDS RETURN MEN HATRED
## FOR CONTEMPT...

Weak minds return men hatred for contempt,
Strong ones contempt for hatred. Which is best?

## GUIZOT'S DISGUISE

Guizot, in haste to cut and run,
A lackey's livery has put on;
But whosoever calls *disguise*
In him the lackey's livery, lies.

Guizot resigned office two days before the abdication of Louis
Philippe and escaped to England in disguise.

## TO MISS ISABELLA PERCY

If that old hermit laid to rest
    Beneath your chapel-floor,
Could leave the regions of the blest
    And visit earth once more:
If human sympathies could warm
    His tranquil breast again,
Your innocence that breast could charm,
    Perhaps your beauty pain.

## WHY DO I PRAISE A PEACH...?

    Why do I praise a peach
Not on my wall, no, nor within my reach?
    Because I see the bloom
And scent the fragrance many steps from home.
    Permit me stil to praise
The higher Genius of departed days.
    Some are there yet who, nurst
In the same clime, are vigorous as the first,
    And never waste their hours
(Ardent for action) among meadow flowers.
    Greece with calm eyes I see,
Her pure white marbles have not blinded me,
But breathe on me the love
Of earthly things as bright as things above:
    There is (where is there not?)
In her fair regions many a desart spot;
    Neither is Dircè clear,
Nor is Ilissus full throughout the year.


## 'TWAS FAR BEYOND THE
## MIDNIGHT HOUR...

'Twas far beyond the midnight hour
    And more than half the stars were falling,
And jovial friends, who lost the power
    Of sitting, under chairs lay sprawling;

Not Porson so; his stronger pate
    Could carry more of wine and Greek
Than Cambridge held; erect he sate;
    He nodded, yet could somehow speak.

"'Tis well, O Bacchus! they are gone,
    Unworthy to approach thy altar!
The pious man prays best alone,
    Nor shall thy servant ever falter.'

Then Bacchus too, like Porson, nodded,
    Shaking the ivy on his brow,
And graciously replied the Godhead,
    'I have no votary staunch as thou.'


## PROPHECY

The Mexicans will flay the Spaniards
And throw their skins into the tan-yards;
The tawny tribes around will wrench
Their beards and whiskers off the French,
And, after a good hearty scourging,
Devote them to the Blessed Virgin.


## DIRCE

Stand close around, ye Stygian set,
    With Dirce in one boat conveyed!
Or Charon, seeing, may forget
    That he is old and she a shade.


## SOMETIMES A JESUIT'S WORDS
## ARE TRUE...

Sometimes a Jesuit's words are true,
For proof one specimen may do.
'To malice all an ear incline,
Even the few who don't malign.'

Reference is made to a passage in the *De Epigrammate*, etc.,
of Francis Vavassor (died 1681).

## FRENCHMEN

Whiskered Furies! boy-stuft blouses!
Fanning fires on peaceful houses!
What are all these oaths and yells
Belcht from thirty million hells?
Swagger, scream, and *peste* away!
Courage now, anon dismay!
Louis-Philip! rear your walls
Round these madmen and their brawls.
Well you know the fiery rout,
And what rain can put it out.


## TO PORSON

Let alone, my old friend, our best poet; ask Parr
If I keep not stout harness well buckled for war.
Of the birch in my field I have wasted no twig
On a petulant Jeffrey or any such prig;
But run not *you* foul on the wise and the kind,
Or you'll soon have to clap your ten fingers behind.

Lord Jeffrey (1773–1850): Scottish judge and critic, was editor
of the *Edinburgh Review* from 1803 to 1829.

## DYING SPEECH OF AN OLD PHILOSOPHER

I strove with none, for none was worth my strife:
    Nature I loved, and, next to Nature, Art:
I warm'd both hands before the fire of Life;
    It sinks; and I am ready to depart.

This best-known of Landor's poems was written on his seventy-fourth birthday. He still had another fifteen years of life before him.

## EPITAPH

So then at last the emperor Franz,
On spindle shanks hath joined Death's dance.
Prythee, good Saint Nepomucene,
Push the pale wretch behind the screen;—
For if your Master's Son should know,
He'd kick him to the gulph below:
Then would the Devil rave and rant,
That Hell has more than Hell can want
Of such exceedingly good men,
And fork him to you back agen.

Reference is made to Francis I, Emperor of Austria (died 1835).

## THERE ARE A HUNDRED NOW ALIVE...

There are a hundred now alive
Who buz about the summer hive,
Alas! how very few of these
Poor little busy poet bees
Can we expect again to hum
When the next summer shall have come.

## BYRON

Like mad-dog in the hottest day
Byron runs snapping strait away,
And those unlucky fellows judge ill
Who go without a whip or cudgel.

The boots I wear are high and strong,
Wherefore I take no whip or thong;
Yet, I confess it, I am loth,
People should see them daub'd with froth,
Tho' dogs that rave with this disease
Lift not their heads above my knees,
It's prudent not to carry home
The worst of poison in their foam.


## VOLTAIRE

Of those who speak about Voltaire
The least malicious are unfair.
The groundlings neither heed nor know
The victories of Apollo's bow;

What powers of darkness he withstood
And stampt upon the Python's brood.
Observing still his easy pace,
They call it levity, not grace.

## VISCOUNT MELVILLE

God's laws declare,
Thou shalt not swear
By aught in heaven above or earth below.
*Upon my honour!* Melville cries...
He swears, and lies...
Does Melville then break God's commandment? No.

Henry Dundas, first Viscount Melville (1742–1811): impeached
for malversation in 1806, he was found guilty of negligence only,
and acquitted.

## DEATH, IN APPROACHING, BRINGS ME SLEEP SO SOUND...

Death, in approaching, brings me sleep so sound
I scarcely hear the dreams that hover round;
One cruel thing, one only, he can do...
Break the bright image (Life's best gift) of you.

## SIR WALTER SCOTT

Ye who have lungs to mount the Muse's hill,
Here slake your thirst aside their liveliest rill:
Asthmatic Wordsworth, Byron piping-hot,
Leave in the rear, and march with manly Scott.

## FOR A GRAVESTONE IN SPAIN

Say thou who liest here beneath,
To fall in battle is not death.
You, tho' no pall on you was cast,
Heard the first trump nor fear'd the last.

The Spanish uprising of 1808 against Napoleon's interference,
curiously paralleling the events of a hundred and twenty-five
years later, excited widespread sympathy and enthusiasm in this
country. Among the volunteers to the Spanish army was
Landor. But the mismanagement of the affairs with which he
had passionately identified himself, disgusted and irritated him
to such an extent that he returned after only three months, with
little to show for his adventure but a depleted purse and an
honorary colonelcy in the Spanish army.

## TO MACAULAY

The dreamy rhymer's measured snore
Falls heavy on our ears no more;
And by long strides are left behind
The dear delights of woman-kind,
Who win their battles like their loves,
In satin waistcoats and kid gloves,
And have achieved the crowning work
When they have truss'd and skewer'd a Turk.
Another comes with stouter tread,
And stalks among the statelier dead.
He rushes on, and hails by turns
High-crested Scott, broad-breasted Burns,
And shows the British youth, who ne'er
Will lag behind, what Romans were,
When all the Tuscans and their Lars
Shouted, and shook the towers of Mars.

70

## TO POETS

Patience! coy songsters of the Delphic wood,
The brightest sun tempts forth the viper brood;
And, of all insects buds and blooms enclose,
The one that stinks the most infests the rose.

## SINGLETON

One leg across his wide arm-chair,
Sat Singleton, and read Voltaire;
And when (as well he might) he hit
Upon a splendid piece of wit,
He cried: 'I do declare now, this
Upon the whole is not amiss.'
And spent a good half-hour to show
By metaphysics why 'twas so.

## SMILES SOON ABATE...

Smiles soon abate; the boisterous throes
    Of anger long burst forth;
Inconstantly the south-wind blows,
    But steadily the north.

Thy star, O Venus! often changes
    Its radiant seat above,
The chilling pole-star never ranges—
    'Tis thus with Hate and Love.

## TO AN OLD POET

'Turn on the anvil twice or thrice
Your verse', was Horace's advice:
Religiously you follow that,
And hammer it til cold and flat.

## SEEN AT ROME

A good old Englishwoman, who had come
Back to her country from the sights at Rome,
Was askt about them.
               'Well then, I have seen
Robes on men's shoulders rich as round our queen...
Strangers, who know no better, may miscall
A well-stuft strutting sausage *cardinal*:
It is not often we so gut a name,
But *cardinal* and *carnal* are the same.'


## GIBBON

Gibbon! tho' thou art grave and grand
And Rome is under thy command,
Yet some in cauliflower-white wigs,
Others put lately into brigs,
Instead of bending back and knee,
Would pull thy chair from under thee.


## TO MATHIAS

The Piper's music fills the street,
The Piper's music makes the heat
   Hotter by ten degrees:
Hand us a Sonnet, dear Mathias,
Hand us a Sonnet cool and dry as
   Your very best, and we shall freeze.

T. J. Mathias (1754?–1835): librarian at Buckingham Palace,
satirist, translator, and Italian scholar.

## *for an* EPITAPH AT FIESOLE

Lo! where the four mimosas blend their shade,
In calm repose at last is Landor laid;
For ere he slept he saw them planted here
By her his soul had ever held most dear,
And he had lived enough when he had dried her tear.

In a letter to his sisters, dated January 1830, Landor wrote: 'In
a few days, whenever the weather will allow it, I have four
mimosas ready to place round my intended tomb, and a friend
who is coming to plant them.' The friend was Ianthe, who had
come to Florence with her children the previous year. Landor
was destined never to be laid in this grave.

## NEVER MUST MY BONES BE LAID...

Never must my bones be laid
Under the mimosa's shade.
He to whom I gave my all
Swept away her guardian wall,
And her green and level plot
Green or level now is not.

The references in this poem, which was written during Landor's
last years in Italy, are to Arnold and Ianthe.

## ONE LOVELY NAME ADORNS
## MY SONG...

One lovely name adorns my song,
And, dwelling in the heart,
For ever falters at the tongue,
And trembles to depart.

# IN CLEMENTINA'S ARTLESS MIEN...

In Clementina's artless mien
   Lucilla asks me what I see
And are the roses of sixteen
   Enough for me?

Lucilla asks, if that be all,
   Have I not cull'd as sweet before...
Ah yes, Lucilla! and their fall
   I still deplore.

I now behold another scene,
   Where Pleasure beams with heaven's own light,
More pure, more constant, more serene,
   And not less bright...

Faith, on whose breast the Loves repose,
   Whose chain of flowers no force can sever,
And Modesty who, when she goes,
   Is gone for ever.

## TO CARY

On his Appointment to a low office in the
British Museum.

Cary! I fear the fruits are scanty
Thou gatherest from the fields of Dante,
But thou hast found at least a shed
Wherin to cram thy truckle-bed;
The porter's lodge of the Museum
May daily hear thee sing *Te Deum*.

Peaches and grapes are mostly found
Richest the nearest to the ground:
Our gardeners take especial care
To keep down low all boughs that bear.
Dante's long labyrinthine line
Is straiten'd and drawn tight by thine:
Hell, devil, dog, in force remain,
And Paradise blooms fresh again.

Henry Francis Cary (1772–1844): translator of Dante, Pindar
and Aristophanes, was given an appointment in the British
Museum Library in 1826. He and Landor had been fellow
scholars at Rugby.

## ON GOETHE'S EPIGRAMS

The *Revelations* want a guide
To draw the mystic veil aside;
For these perhaps one guide may do,
But Goethe's *Epigrames* want two.

## A POET SLEEPING

The poet sleeps: at every wheeze,
   At every grunt and groan
You cry, 'His verses how like these!
   He marks them for his own.'

## TO A GERMAN

You think all liquor must be weak if clear,
Find wit in Goethe, miss it in Voltaire.
Your beer has plenty both of malt and hop,
But of the bright and sparkling not a drop.

## THE FARMER THEOLOGIAN'S
## HARANGUE

Good people! I wonder now what ye are a'ter,
Who made such a bother o' late about water;
Whether children on whom not a drop ever fell
Could escape, good or naughty, the torments of hell.
While one wants it fresh and while one wants it salt,
I advise you to give it a slight dash of malt.


## ON A LADY'S SURPRISE AT MY
## IGNORANCE OF BOTANY

Instead of idling half my hours,
I might have learnt the names of flowers
    In gardens, groves, and fields:
But where had been the sweet surprise,
That sparkles from those dark-blue eyes?
    Less pleasure knowledge yields.


## EPIGRAM

Expect no grape, no fig, no wholesome fruit
From Gaul engrafted upon Corsican.

Landor, like Beethoven and many of his contemporaries, had
had great hopes for the libertarian outcome of the French
Revolution; but, with the acquisition of dictatorial powers by
Napoleon, his early enthusiasm turned to hate and denunciation.

# TO THE COUNTESS OF BLESSINGTON

Since in the terrace-bower we sate
　　While Arno gleam'd below,
And over sylvan Massa late
　　Hung Cynthia's slender bow,
Years after years have past away
　　Less light and gladsome; why
Do those we most implore to stay
　　Run ever swiftest by!

Lady Blessington (1789–1849): author of a number of novels, no longer readable, and editor of *The Book of Beauty*. Landor first met Lord and Lady Blessington while they were visiting Florence in 1827, and accompanied them on an excursion to Naples. During the Bath period it was his habit to spend a week or two nearly every year with Lady Blessington and Count D'Orsay at Gore House.

## BURNS

Had we two met, blythe-hearted Burns,
　　Tho water is my daily drink,
　　May God forgive me but I think
We should have roared our toasts by turns.

Inquisitive low-whispering cares
　　Had found no room in either pate,
　　Until I asked thee, rather late,
Is there a hand-rail to the stairs?

Burns died when Landor was twenty-one.

## MISTAKE RECTIFIED

'Tis not Lucilla that you see
　　Amid the cloud and storm:
'Tis Anger.... What a shame that he
　　Assumes Lucilla's form!

## ADVICE TO AN OLD POET

After edition comes edition,
    And scarce a dozen copies gone;
Suppose you take another 'mission'
    And let the weary press alone.


## IN EARLY SPRING...

In early spring, ere roses took
A matronly unblushing look,
Or lilies had begun to fear
A stain upon their character,
I thought the cuckoo more remote
Than ever, and more hoarse his note.
The nightingale had dropt one half
Of her large gamut, and the laugh
Of upright nodding woodpecker
Less petulantly struck my ear.
Why have the birds forgot to sing
In this as in a former spring?
Can it be that the days are cold.
Or (surely not) that I am old.
Strange fancy! how could I forget
That I have not seen eighty yet!


## *from* CATULLUS, CARMEN XIII

With me, Fabullus, you shall dine,
    And gaudily, I promise you,
If you will only bring the wine,
    The dinner, and some beauty too.

With all your frolic, all your fun,
   I have some little of my own;
And nothing else: the spiders run
   Throughout my purse, now theirs alone.


## ON SOUTHEY'S TOMB

Few tears, nor those too warm, are shed
By poet over poet dead.
Without premeditated lay
To catch the crowd, I only say,
As over Southey's slab I bend,
The best of mortals was my friend.

The life-long friendship between Landor and Southey began
in 1808. This epitaph, despite its title, does not appear upon
Southey's tomb.


## EPITHALAMIUM

   Weep Venus, and ye
   Adorable Three
Who Venus for ever environ!
   Pounds shillings and pence
   And shrewd sober sense
Have clapt the strait waistcoat on...

   Off, Mainot and Turk,
   With pistol and dirk,
Nor palace nor pinnace set fire on:
   The cord's fatal jerk
   Has done its last work,
And the noose is now slipt upon...

## FUGITIVE PIECES

Fugitive pieces! no indeed,
How can those be whose feet are lead?

## TRELAWNY

It is not every traveler
Who like Trelawny can aver
In every State he left behind
An image the Nine Months may find.

Considerate, he perceived the need
Of some improvement in the breed,
And set as heartily to work
As when he fought against the Turk.

Edward John Trelawny (1792–1881): writer, explorer and adventurer. He was present at Leghorn when Shelley was drowned, and fought with Byron in the Greek war for independence. Wild exploits (such as swimming across Niagara), and his association with Byron, led to his being energetically lionised by London society.

## SIR CHARLES NAPIER

How could you think to conquer Scinde,
And leave no enemy behind?
Indus rolls onward fifty streams,
But none so noisome as the Thames.

## SENT WITH FLOWERS

Take the last flowers your natal day
    May ever from my hand receive!
Sweet as the former ones are they,
    And sweet alike be those they leave.

Another in the year to come
　　May offer them to smiling eyes;
The smile that cannot reach my tomb
　　Will add fresh radiance to the skies.


## THERMOMETER

If the Rhætian Alps of old
Were insufferably cold,
Colder ten degrees are they
Since Reade's Poems blew that way,
And those bleak and steril scalps
Now are call'd the Readian Alps.

John Edmund Reade (1800–70): poetaster, novelist, and fore-
most plagiarist of his time, was the butt of several sarcastic
poems by Landor.


## FORSTER! COME HITHER...

Forster! come hither, I pray, to the Fast of our Anglican
　　Martyr.
Turbot our Church has allow'd, and perhaps (not without
　　dispensation)
Pheasant; then strawberry cream, green-gages, and apricot-
　　jelly,
Oranges housewives call *pot*, and red-rinded nuts of Avella,
Filberts we name them at home—happy they who have teeth
　　for the crackers!
Blest, but in lower degree, whose steel-arm'd right-hand
　　overcomes them!
I, with more envy than spite, look on and sip sadly my claret.

John Forster: a friend and contemporary of Dickens, appointed
by Landor to be his official biographer and literary executor.

## INOPPORTUNE

A crunching bear inopportunely bit
    Thy finger, Reade!
It should have been ere thy first verse was writ,
    It should indeed!


## THE SCRIPTURES TEACH US...

The scriptures teach us that our Lord
Writes in his book man's idlest word.
Now surely he must find it worse
Than what he suffered on the cross.

In evil hour I strove to read
Some poems of one lately dead,
And humbly hoped the sable pall
Might cover and atone for all.


## WAR IN CHINA

There may be many reasons why,
O ancient land of Kong-Fu-Tsi!
Some fain would make the little feet
Of thy indwellers run more fleet.
But while, as now, before my eyes
The steams of thy sweet herb arise,
Amid bright vestures, faces fair,
Long eyes, and closely braided hair,
And many a bridge and many a barge,
And many a child and bird as large,
I cannot wish thee wars nor woes...
And when thy lovely single rose,
Which every morn I haste to see,
Smiles with fresh-opened flower on me,

And when I think what hand it was
Cradled the nursling in its vase,
By all thy Gods!  O ancient land!
I wish thee and thy laws to stand.


## TO LESBIA

*(Imitations from* CATULLUS, III)

Yes! my Lesbia! let us prove
All the sweets of life in love.
Let us laugh at envious sneers;
Envy is the fault of years.
Vague report let us despise;
Suns may set and suns may rise:
We, when sets *our* twinkling light,
Sleep a long-continued night.
Make we then, the most of this—
Let us kiss, and kiss, and kiss.
While we thus the night employ,
Envy cannot know our joy.
So, my Lesbia! let us prove
All the sweets of life in love.


## IDLE AND LIGHT...

Idle and light are many things you see
In these my closing pages: blame not me.
However rich and plenteous the repast,
Nuts, almonds, biscuits, wafers, come at last.

## YEARS, MANY PARTI-COLOR'D YEARS...

Years, many parti-color'd years,
  Some have crept on, and some have flown,
Since first before me fell those tears
  I never could see fall alone.

Years, not so many, are to come,
  Years not so varied, when from you
One more will fall: when, carried home,
  I see it not, nor hear *adieu*!

## TO A POET

I never call'd thy Muse splay-footed,
Who sometimes wheez'd, and sometimes hooted,
As owls do on a lonely tower,
Awaiting that propitious hour
When singing birds retire to rest,
And owls may pounce upon the nest.
I only wish she would forbear
From sticking pins into my chair,
And let alone the friends who come
To neutralize thy laudanum.

## TO A DOG

Giallo! I shall not see thee dead,
Nor raise a stone above thy head,
For I shall go some years before,
Where thou wilt leap at me no more,

Nor bark, as now, to make me mind,
Asking me, am I deaf or blind:
No, Giallo, but I shall be soon,
And thou wilt scratch my turf and moan.

Giallo, a Pomeranian like Pomero, was Landor's pet during the
final period at Florence. He survived his master by eight years.

## TO AGE

Welcome, old friend! These many years
   Have we lived door by door:
The Fates have laid aside their shears
   Perhaps for some few more.

I was indocil at an age
   When better boys were taught,
But thou at length hast made me sage,
   If I am sage in aught.

Little I know from other men,
   Too little they from me,
But thou hast pointed well the pen
   That writes these lines to thee.

Thanks for expelling Fear and Hope,
   One vile, the other vain;
One's scourge, the other's telescope,
   I shall not see again:

Rather what lies before my feet
   My notice shall engage...
He who hath braved Youth's dizzy heat
   Dreads not the frost of Age.

## THE GRATEFUL HEART

The grateful heart for all things blesses;
  Not only joy, but grief endears:
I love you for your few caresses,
  I love you for my many tears.

# INDEX OF FIRST LINES

89

Printed in the United States
By Bookmasters